Writing Prompts:
Sixty Days of Mystery and Mayhem

J.W. Nicholson

This is a work of fiction. Names, characters, places, and incident either are the product of the author's imagination or are used fictitiously, and any resemblance to any persons, living or dead, business establishments, events, or locales is entirely
coincidental.

Writing Prompts: Sixty Days of Mystery and Mayhem

Published by CreateSpace Publishers

First Printing: March 2017
Printed in the United States of America

First Edition: March, 2017

Writing Prompts:

Sixty Days of Mystery and Mayhem

Writing Prompts: Sixty Days of Mystery and Mayhem is meant to guide you on a journey of sixty days of writing. Whether you are wanting to establish a healthy writing habit or you just want to gain a new perspective. Or, maybe you just want a jump start writing mysteries. Whatever the reason that you have started on this journey, I'm glad you have. I've been where you are. Just wanting a little inspiration. Then again, maybe it is a fun way to pass the time.

For the next sixty days your characters will be placed in mysterious and dangerous situations. And it is your job to write their stories. Write them anyway you want. The questions that I present to you are just starting points for you and your characters. In the writing prompts, I may refer to the hero as he, but you most certainly can plug in the hero as a she. It is your story, your words, and your characters. If at any point you feel a book welling up with any of these ideas, feel free to use the ideas in your book in any way. My hope is that this jumps starts you to write, and that you write often. Now get to writing!

Day 1

Your character is in the middle of nowhere and his car has quit. The only place nearby is a shady motel with a vacancy light on. Wolves howl in the distance. A car with a blaring radio passes by. What happens
next?

Brainstorm Here

Day 2

The hero finds himself in a quiet little town, miles away from big city. He enters many businesses, but no one is there. Strange. About an hour after he arrives, he hears a woman screaming. It is up to you to write what has happened in this peculiar town.

Brainstorm Here

Day 3

Your character has been put in charge of investigating an
animal attack in Wyoming. Locals are convinced it is not an
animal that has done these vile deeds. Your
character isn't convinced that it is an animal attack either, but
what could it be?

Brainstorm Here

Day 4

Your character wakes up in a field with no
recollection of what has happened in his life for the last year.
The only item that is familiar to him is the necklace he's
wearing. Write a story of what has happened to him or her.

Brainstorm Here

Day 5

Your character has been thrown in a waterfall. It is up to you to decide the location. Amazon? Mountains? Hawaii? Tell the story of how he survives or how he doesn't.

Brainstorm Here

Day 6

It's a damp, dark night in October. Your character is in quite a predicament. He has been locked in a coffin. Will he find a way out or stare death in the face? The choice is yours. Things to think about are:
Who put him in the coffin?
Will he escape and how?

Brainstorm Here

Day 7

Your character is on a cruise when he notices that the number of people on the ship has decreased dramatically. None of the crew seems to notice. It is only the passengers that become alarmed. How does your character react to the situation? Perhaps pirates have taken over. Or, maybe it's a ghost ship. Tell your story.

Brainstorm Here

Day 8

Your character is a member of the town council. In the previous weeks, he has found mistakes in the accounting. Large amounts of money have disappeared. He finds it strange that no other member of the council has discovered these mistakes. And the two times he has mentioned it to the members they have told him he must have calculated wrong. They inform him he needs to leave the accounting to the professionals. How will your character solve the mystery of the missing money?

Brainstorm Here

Day 9

Your character is tied to a tree in an open field. The only objects he can see in his point of view are the pine trees at the horizon line and a duffel bag to his right which isn't his.

Brainstorm Here

Day 10

The hero has been left to die in a swamp in the Mississippi Delta. He has a bullet wound and needs medical attention. But right now the alligator swimming toward him is his greatest concern. What will happen to the hero? Only you can decide.

Brainstorm Here

New Orleans is the perfect setting for a mystery, and that is just where your hero finds himself next. Amongst the Oak trees and Spanish moss are the "Cities of the Dead", the great cemeteries of New Orleans. It is in one of the white washed tombs, perhaps even the voodoo queens, your hero finds himself. Only you know why he is there, and what will happen next.

Brainstorm Here

Day 12

The hero passed a man with a trench coat and a violinist before he hopped on the subway. That was two hours ago. Now the hero has a bomb strapped to him on the New York City subway. Did he have it strapped to him before he entered the station or did someone strap it to him on the subway?
Write away.

Brainstorm Here

Your character has taken a vacation. He has decided to ride to a ghost town that he had seen on one of the pamphlets back at the hotel. At first, it looks like what he would imagine a ghost town to look like. Abandoned buildings. Broken windows. Ropes hanging looped on the sides of the buildings. Yep everything thing looks normal for a ghost town until your boy steps out to the barn. There he discovers a group of peo- ple that are currently inhabiting the barn. After talking with the people for a while, he discovers that they are obviously some kind of cult. What happens next is up to you. Does your hero head back to the hotel? Does he get kidnapped by the cult leader? Does he call the police? Tell the story how you see it.

Brainstorm Here

Day 14

Your character walks into a convenience store that is currently being robbed. Just as he walks in a shot is fired. There is one female clerk. The cash register is opened and an eleven year old boy is standing in the chip aisle. Continue the story.

Brainstorm Here

Day 15

Place the hero in a brewery barrel. No one knows he is there. The hero is best friends with the guy who owns the brewery. There is one employee on duty where the barrel is. But the employee is on the other side of the room and makes no move as the hero screams. Can the employee hear the hero? Did the employee put the hero in the barrel? Only you can discover the truth.

Brainstorm Here

Day 16

Place the hero in a hearse. Is he driving? Is he in the coffin? Is he a pallbearer? It's your story, it's up to you.

Brainstorm Here

Day 17

Your character finds himself in the cold, dank morgue located
in the basement of the hospital.

Brainstorm Here

Day 18

Your hero is irrationally afraid of spiders. It's no secret. Many people in his life know this fact about him. Today, your hero answered the door only to receive a box of spiders from FedEx. Who would do this to him and why? You write the rest.

Brainstorm Here

Day 19

The hero has been locked in an antebellum house in
Savannah, Georgia that is believed to be
haunted. Your hero doesn't believe in ghost, but he can't
deny the strange things that keep happening to him. Not to
mention the fact that he can't open the door or break through
any of the windows. It's your job to come up with what is going
on in this house.

Brainstorm Here

Day 20

Water is dripping. The sounds of cars passing on the highway are faint. And your hero is locked in a basement. It smells musty and there is only one window. Decide how your character got here. Will he escape? Only you know what his fate is. Write. Write. Write.

Brainstorm Here

Your character is surrounded by gurneys, old medical equipment, and tools. Don't forget the cement walls. Have you
guessed it yet? Yes. No. Your character is in an abandoned
hospital, and you get to write a story of how he came to be
in the hospital. Or maybe you want to write about what happened to the hospital. Why was all the medical equipment
left behind? Write Away.

Brainstorm Here

Day 22

All your character knows is he's woke up by the ocean in the middle of the night. He has no wallet. His car is gone, and he has this strange tattoo on his arm. There's a couple of love birds on a pier, and a late night jogger. On day 22, your assignment is to give this wayward soul a story.

Brainstorm Here

Day 23

The smell of fish fills your character's nostrils. He can hear yelling along the wharf. And he hears and smells all this from inside the shipping container that he has been hurled into. A shipping container that is filled with a dozen other people. Your prompt today is to give a voice to their story.

Brainstorm Here

A carnival has come to town. Your character is a dectective, and he has been sent to investigate the disappearance of three of the Carnival people. Your prompt is to tell the events that led up to now, and the mystery that makes up their stories.

Brainstorm Here

How did your hero wind up in a cave? Not only is he in a cave he is blindfolded. And not only is he in a cave blindfolded, but the cave is filled with snakes. Seems someone has played a cruel joke on your hero. And you are about to tell the story of just how all of this came about.

Brainstorm Here

Day 26

The mother of the hero has went on a vacation. She promised to call him when she arrived at her hotel in Scottsdale. But it's been twenty-four hours, and he hasn't heard from her. He can't reach her on her cell phone either. He just can't shake the feeling that something is not right. This is where you come in. Write about what has happened to the mother.

Brainstorm Here

Day 27

Your hero is a farmer, and he arrived at work only to find a body under one of his combines that was left in the soybean field. What is going on in this farmer's fields? Fill in the missing gaps to this farmer mystery.

Brainstorm Here

Day 28

The door is locked. The television is blaring in the neighbor's room, and your hero is trapped in his motel room. Talk about a vacation gone wrong. Your hero can't seem to catch a break. Oh well, at least it gives you plenty to write about. In this prompt write about this bizarre hotel and your hero's misfortune.

Brainstorm Here

Day 29

Your hero is a journalist, and a kidnapper has just fed live feed of your hero's family to him on live television and asked for a ransom. If your hero doesn't come up with the ransom by tomorrow, the kidnapper will execute your hero's entire family on live stream.

Brainstorm Here

Day 30

Your hero is twelve years old, and has just been
kidnapped by human traffickers. Tell his experience.

Brainstorm Here

Day 31

The hero unknowingly takes a job with the head boss of a drug cartel. When he finds out, it is too late. He is drowning in debt, and really needs the job.

Brainstorm Here

The hero's car quits on a desolate highway, and an old man in a pickup gives your hero a ride. The old man takes your hero back to his house with the promise that he can use his house phone to call a tow service. When they arrive at the old man's house, your hero notices pictures of young men around his age. Different men. It's at that moment he's realizes he's made a grave mistake. This is where your story picks up.

Brainstorm Here

Day 33

In today's writing prompt your hero is a real estate agent that is trying to sell a house that is haunted. Every time he shows the house to someone something happens to scare them away. Cabinets move on their own. Doors slam. Write this as scary or as funny as you want.

Brainstorm Here

Day 34

Your hero lives in a world where strange happenings are an everyday occurrence. Today, an entire town has vanished, and it is your hero's job to figure out what has happened to them.

Brainstorm Here

Day 35

Your character is a detective, a FBI agent, or a Policeman. Today, he has taken a day off work to go fishing. He has been fishing at a lake for nearly two hours when he sees a body floating nearby. He grabs his cell phone that he had turned off and calls it in. Feel free to write about the events that led up to the body floating in the water or the events after or anything in between.

Brainstorm Here

Day 36

Clank! Bang! Your hero is remodeling a house that he just closed on last week. He's decided to tear down the wall that divides the kitchen from the living room to make the house more open. The smell of coffee fills the room. The construction guys are busy at work when one of them yells. The hero walks over to the crew to see what all the fuss is about, and that's when he sees the skeleton through the broken sheetrock. Now, you tell the rest of the story. It can include as much of the story of how the skeleton came to be there as you want. That's the great thing about it being your story, you can spin it however you want.

Brainstorm Here

Day 37

The sun rays blind your hero as he begins to wake up. He rubs his eyes. He smells the faint smell of metallic. His head throbs. He pulls back the covers. That's when he sees his body covered in blood. He does a quick inventory of his body and realizes it's not his blood that he's covered with. Now, you take the story and run with it.

Brainstorm Here

Day 38

As your character walks through the busy streets, the smell of curry and garlic overwhelm him. Blue, purple, and red blur past him. His eyes scan the busy Indian market. He must find her. But he has yet to see her. Who does he need to find? Why does he need to find her? Why is he in India? These are questions that only you can answer.

Brainstorm Here

Day 39

Your hero is having a lunch date with a friend. His friend has ordered a salad. When the food arrives, the friends stabs the fork in the salad and screams. Your hero looks over to see why his friend screamed, and there in the middle of the salad is a finger. Whose finger is it? What happened? How will your hero handle the situation? What will the friend do?

Brainstorm Here

Day 40

Escape Rooms are all the rage now. People willingly put down cash to solve a good mystery. Here's a thought. What if your hero went with some friends to one of the hour long entertainment games? And what if after an hour it kept going and going and going? What would this story look like? What would happen? Would people take your hero and his buddies in a black sedan to a secret location as a continuation of the game? It's up to you as to what happens in this mystery.

Brainstorm Here

Day 41

Your character is a logger. He spends most of his day in the great outdoors. He is working on the most remote worksite that he has ever been on. So remote, that no one lives around for miles and miles. As he operates the Caterpillar, he notices what looks like a primitive village in the distance. He's been told that the property is privately owned, and no one has inhabited this place since the 1800s. What happens next? Tell the story of the village. Tell the story of the logger.

Brainstorm Here

Your character doesn't know his neighbors very well. Infact, he's been known to be pompous to them quite often. It could be that your character has been rude one too many times to the neighborhood. At work your character receives a phone call from the school saying his daughter is missing. While he is on the phone with the school, he receives a second call. The second call is none other than a ticked off neighbor who has kidnapped his daughter and is asking for ransom money. Write the story.

Brainstorm Here

Day 43

Kidneys being stolen are an urban legend. Right?
Maybe if it's a motel with a bathtub filled with ice. But what if
your hero woke up in a hospital where a doctor had removed
his kidney without his permission? And what if all the precau-
tions had been taken with the hospital in order for the sur-
gery to occur? But now the doctor, nor the surgical nurse that
helped to perform the operation, nor the person whom they
placed your character's kidney into can be found. They have
simply disappeared. How will you write this story?

Brainstorm Here

Day 44

A letter arrives at the hero's house telling him he has three days to find a rare painting or his wife will be killed.

Brainstorm Here

Day 45

A body is found in the hero's bathtub.
Electrocution is the cause of death. Your hero has never seen
the person before, but all the evidence is pointing to him.
Looks like someone wants to frame your hero. Who? Why?
What's the story

Brainstorm Here

Day 46

Cheerleaders are disappearing from the local
high school. Three have disappeared in the last two days. No
one has any idea what is happening. Write a story about the
disappearance of the small town cheerleaders.

Brainstorm Here

Day 47

The hero's spouse has been mailed love letters with the words cut out of newspapers. The letters contain intimate details of their lives along with photographs. Who is sending these love letters and why?

Brainstorm Here

Day 48

Someone has set up video cameras in the hero's house. Watching intimate details of his life. Who would want to do such a thing and why? Tell the story.

Brainstorm Here

Day 49

Your characters phones are being tapped by his ex-girlfriend or boyfriend. Lately your character feels like someone is watching him/her. What happens? Is the ex bitter? Tell their story.

Brainstorm Here

Day 50

Your character finds himself tied to a chair in the middle of a warehouse. Cars of all kinds surround him in various states of disrepair. He can see a man busy taking a license plate off a Porsche. Write a story about what happened prior to your character winding up here or what happens next or both.

Brainstorm Here

Your hero walks into the red, brick bank and meets in a closed room with his banker then leaves. Thirty minutes later the banker is found with a knife in his chest lying on the floor. Your hero was the last one to be seen with him or so the loan secretary stated? Write this story.

Brainstorm Here

Day 52

The branch doesn't look like it will hold him for long. Your character finds himself hanging above a pit of what looks like hungry alligators. How did he come about being here? Is there anyone here with him or is he alone? Write. Write. Write.

Brainstorm Here

Day 53

The sound of metal clanging against metal can be heard. People yelling over the sounds of machinery and your hero just happens to be in the trunk of a car about to be crushed at a junkyard. He screams, but no one seems to hear him. What will happen next?

Brainstorm Here

Day 54

This morning started like any other morning. Your hero got up. He got ready for work. He ate his breakfast. Then he took out his trash. This was his mistake. Someone was waiting for him at the trash bin. And now, your hero finds himself in a basement with this mad woman or man. Write their story.

Brainstorm Here

Day 55

The hero has been injected with lethal poison and has three
hours to live. Who gave him the injection? Why did they give
him the injection? Show in your own words what is
happening.

Brainstorm Here

Day 56

Ever feel it's going to be one of those days? You know the one where nothing seems to go right. Your sock has a hole in it. Your hair won't go down no matter how many times you wet it. That's just the kind of day that your hero seems to be having today. And to top it all off someone tied a cement block to his feet and threw him in the water. What happens next is up to you.

Brainstorm Here

Day 57

What is your characters ultimate fear? Is it snakes? Spiders? Clowns? Roaches? Whatever his fear is, today lock him up in a room with that fear and throw away the key. And then write about it.

Brainstorm Here

Day 58

The wind is blowing hard. All your hero can see for miles is buildings. Skyscrapers. Apartment buildings. And your hero just happens to be on the highest one of them all. It wouldn't be so bad if he weren't being held over the edge by a man that goes by the name of Tiny. It seems he always winds up in the most dangerous predicaments. Once again, this is what has happened. How did he get here? Where are they? What does he hear? What does he see?

Brainstorm Here

Day 59

The character doesn't like the looks of this place. Barbed wire surrounds the perimeter. There are bars on the windows. And he has to leave his mother in this place. He can't see after her, and he can't leave her by herself. She's been cutting her hair, pounding her hammer into the wall because she hears voices, and she's trying to find them. He doesn't know what else to do and he's been told that Harbor House is the best. So, it is here that he leaves his frail mother. And it is here that your story begins.

Brainstorm Here

Day 60

Your character has fallen in love. After two years of being a widow, he has finally found love again. But here is the twist. Your character has unknowingly fallen for the murderer of his deceased spouse. Write this story.

Brainstorm Here

Extra Day

The doorbell rings. Your hero opens the door. A box sits in front of the door. The hero picks up the box and lays it on the table. He hurries back to the bathroom to get ready. Just before walking out of the bathroom there is an explosion that knocks your hero across the bathroom, and he hits the wall.
    Write the story of your hero and the mysterious package.

Brainstorm Here

Congratulations! You have wrote for sixty-one consecutive days.

www.ingramcontent.com/pod-product-compliance
Lightning Source LLC
Chambersburg PA
CBHW030526290526
45786CB00004B/1635